DevOps for Beginners:

Hands-on Guide

By David Johnson

Table of Contents

Introduction   5

Chapter 1- What is DevOps?   6

Chapter 2- How to Run a Linux Web
Server on Android Device   8

Chapter 3- Deployment of a Ruby App
with Ansible   15

Chapter 4- A Gift-Flow Releasing Model   44

Chapter 5- Setting Up and Configuring
Jenkins for the Team   61

Chapter 6- How to Prepare and Secure
Ubuntu Box for Deployment   75

Chapter 7- Enabling Virtualization in
ESXi virtual machine   88

Chapter 8- Securing Deployment
Secrets with vault   91

Chapter 9- Tree Structures and
MongoDB   107

Conclusion   121

Disclaimer

While all attempts have been made to verify the information provided in this book, the author does assume any responsibility for errors, omissions, or contrary interpretations of the subject matter contained within. The information provided in this book is for educational and entertainment purposes only. The reader is responsible for his or her own actions and the author does not accept any responsibilities for any liabilities or damages, real or perceived, resulting from the use of this information.

The trademarks that are used are without any consent, and the publication of the trademark is without permission or backing by the trademark owner. All trademarks and brands within this book are for clarifying purposes only and are the owned by the owners themselves, not affiliated with this document.

Introduction

It is essential to be able to organize the members of a software development team in such a way that their operations can run smoothly. The same applies to the operations that are to be done when developing software. This book is a guide for you on how to achieve that. Enjoy reading!

Chapter 1- What is DevOps?

DevOps represents a way in which a team can be organized. In this case, the team will be working to deliver a particular piece of software, and, once delivered; maximum functionality will be expected from it. No pre-specified way to do DevOps exists: there is no pre-defined method by which a DevOps team can be organized to work efficiently. The approach is a philosophy, meaning that it is a culture and a general approach in which each member of the team has to be willing and appreciate what is being done. If you are pro-DevOps, this is not an indication that each step in the software development process will be defined clearly and finally. The team that is working in the field can choose to be full-on DevOps, or be a little DevOps or be no DevOps at all.

This means that DevOps is just a means of organizing a software development team. A software development process involves developers and operations. The two terms make the

DevOps (Developer Operations). The developers are responsible for the actual process of developing the software, while the operations have to work on a daily basis so as to ensure that the software is in a good working condition. The two groups of people are believed to possess different mindsets. The developers like to make changes, as geared by the innovations that they need to implement, while the operations are adverse to this. A "wall of confusion" usually occurs when the attitudes of the developers and operations differ.

Chapter 2- How to Run a Linux Web Server on Android Device

It is easy for us to run Linux webserver on an android device by using the GNU program, and we will not be expected to root the device. After running Linux, servers such as Sinatra, Rails, Node will be in a position to run the webapps on the localhost. An NPM library named "localtunnel" can help us in exposing the local server to our broader internet. Follow the steps given below:

1. Ensure that your hard disk storage has enough space.

   The Linux OS should take at least 1GB of space in the hard disk, so ensure that you have this. This can also be installed on an OS card, but we don't recommend it because of the inferior performance.

2. Install the GnuRoot Debian.

The Gnu Root is a 60MB download, so download from the link in play store.

3. Install the Linux.

You can then launch the program and click on the option for "install/reinstall". With that, the Linux operating system will be compiled and then installed. The Gnu Root program will be closed once the installation is completed.

Remember that an error exists in the GnuRoot app, in which the terminal window will not show up once it has been back-grounded and then re-opened. For you to re-open the app after back-grounding it, you should press the back button so as to get back to the terminal. If you see the installation screen is empty or black, then this will be an indication that the installation has been completed.

4.   Setup the Linux environment.

Start the GnuRoot app, and then click on the tab for "launch". Start the terminal by clicking on "launch". The first step should be for you to update the package list, which is good for installing the programs. Just execute the following command:

apt-get update

You should also ensure that the OS being run is the current bone, and that it is compatible with the above program list. Upgrade it with the following command:

apt-get upgrade

The next step should involve installation of the necessary tools for the C programming language. This can be accomplished by executing the following command:

apt-get install build-essential

Then execute the following command:

apt-get install ruby ruby-dev

The above will set the commands *"ruby"*, *"irb"*, and *"gem"*. You can then install a   simple web server named "Sinatra". Just execute the following command:

echo "gem: --no-document" >> .gemrc

If you need to prevent the gems from installing the documentation, which might run for a long time, the Sinatra should be installed with the following:

gem install Sinatra

You can then install the NodeJS using the following command:

apt-get install nodejs

In this case, we have just used the normal package for the sake of simplicity, but if you need to, you can use PPA. Some binaries will expect the binary named *"node"*, but in Linux, we normally use *"nodejs"*.

You can then install the Node package manager, the *"NPM"*, using the following command:

apt-get intall npm

For the errors to be preempted, just execute the following command:

ln -s /usr/bin/nodejs /usr/bin/node

With the above command, you will be in a position to use the "*node*" as the alias for "*nodejs*".

astly, you can install the localtunnel using the following command:

npm install -g localtunnel

5.   Write and run the web server.

The first step in this should be writing the instructions for the simple server. Run the following command:

echo "require 'sinatra'; get('/') { 'hello there' }" >> app.rb

The web server can then be run with "***ruby app.rb &***", in which the ampersand (&) represents a background process. The localtunnel listen can be run using the command "*lt --port 4567*", and a url will be printed after some seconds. Copy the url and then open it in your browser. You will see the message *"hello there"*.

Chapter 3- Deployment of a Ruby App with Ansible

Currently, it is easy s to set up a dedicated server and get it running within a few seconds. Everyone will need to make the configurations in the shortest time possible, without having to do it for each server. With a tool named Ansible, this can be automated. Let us discuss how this can be done.

It is good for you to have a basic understanding of the Ansible file syntax. The components to be deployed include Ruby, the application itself and the Web Server with passenger.

Ruby switcher chruby

This is a lightweight tool and easy to understand. The tool can be found at **Github**. Once you master the installation instructions, the manual installation can be automated with Ansible, and then you get a bonus, which is a reusable recipe for installation of "ch_ruby". This is shown below:

```
---

- name: Ruby | Checking if the chruby is present
  shell: test -x /usr/local/bin/chruby-exec
  when: ansible_system == "Linux"
  ignore_errors: yes
  register: chruby_present
  tags: ruby


- name: Ruby | Download the chruby distribution
  get_url:
url="http://github.com/postmodern/chruby/archive/
v{{ chruby_version }}.tar.gz"
```

```
        dest="/tmp/chruby-{{          chruby_version
}}.tar.gz"
  when: chruby_present|failed
  tags: ruby


 - name: Ruby | unpack chruby
   command: tar xf "/tmp/chruby-{{ chruby_version
}}.tar.gz"
       chdir="/tmp"
  when: chruby_present|failed
  tags: ruby
 - name: Ruby | chruby install target
   command: make install
       chdir="/tmp/chruby-{{ chruby_version }}"
  become: yes
  when: chruby_present|failed
  tags: ruby


 - name: Ruby | autoload script
```

```
template:
src="{{role_dir}}/templates/ch_ruby.sh.j2"
dest=/etc/profile.d/chruby.sh

become: yes

tags: ruby
```

Ruby install

The tool Ruby-install can be found from **Github**. Once the setup notes for ruby-install have been studied well, the steps can be automated with ansible steps which are shown below:

```
---

- name: Ruby | Checking if the ruby install is present

  shell: test -x /usr/local/bin/ruby-install

  when: ansible_system == "Linux"

  ignore_errors: yes

  register: rubyinstall_present

  tags: ruby
```

```yaml
- name: Ruby | Ruby install | package dependencies

  apt: pkg={{ item }} state=present force="yes" update_cache="yes"

  when: ansible_system == "Linux"

  with_items:

    - build-essential

    - libffi-dev

    - libgdbm-dev

    - libncurses5-dev

    - libreadline-dev

    - libreadline6-dev

    - libtinfo-dev

    - libyaml-dev

  become: yes

  tags: ruby


- name: Ruby | Download rubyinstall

  get_url: url=http://github.com/postmodern/ruby-install/archive/v{{ ruby_install_version }}.tar.gz
```

```
        dest=/tmp/ruby-install-{{   ruby_install_version
}}.tar.gz
    when: rubyinstall_present | failed
    tags: ruby


  - name: Ruby | Unpack ruby-install
    command: tar xf /tmp/ruby-install-{{
ruby_install_version }}.tar.gz
         chdir=/tmp
    when: rubyinstall_present | failed
    tags: ruby


  - name: Ruby | Run ruby-install install target
    command: make install
         chdir=/tmp/ruby-install-{{ ruby_install_version
}}
    when: rubyinstall_present | failed
    become: yes
    tags: ruby


  - name: Ruby | Download list of rubies available
```

```
command: ruby-install

when: rubyinstall_present | failed

become: yes

tags: ruby
```

Ruby

At this point, you can install Ruby. If the installation is to be done on a shared server, it is a good idea to implement multiple versions of this and implement a mechanism to help you switch between them. The recipe for installation of Ruby should be compact and clear as shown below:

```
---

- name: Ruby | checking out if the ruby_version is installed
  stat:                    path={{rubies_location}}/ruby-{{ruby_version}}
  register: ruby_version_present
```

```yaml
  tags: ruby


- name: Ruby | Install the ruby_version if it's
necessary
  command:        '/usr/local/bin/ruby-install       ruby
{{ruby_version}}'
  when: not ruby_version_present.stat.exists
  become: yes


  tags: ruby


- debug: var="ruby_install_setsystem"
- name: Ruby | Update the SYSTEM ruby_version if
it's necessary
  command: '/usr/local/bin/ruby-install --system
ruby {{ruby_version}}'
  when: option_ruby_install_setsystem
  become: yes
  tags: ruby
```

Webserver & passenger

At this point, we can install the pre-built Nginx with passenger as shown below:

```
---

- name: Nginx | Checking if it is present
  command: test -x /usr/sbin/nginx
  when: ansible_os_family == "Debian"
  ignore_errors: yes
  register: nginx_present
  tags: nginx


- name: Passenger | Adding the GPG key to the apt keyring
  apt_key: keyserver=keyserver.ubuntu.com
  id=561F9B9CAC40B2F7
  when: ansible_os_family == "Debian" and
  nginx_present|failed
  tags: passenger
```

```
become: yes


- name: Passenger | Installing the needed packages

  apt: state=present pkg="{{item}}"

  with_items:

   - apt-transport-https

   - ca-certificates

  when:    ansible_os_family    ==    "Debian"    and

nginx_present|failed

  become: yes

  tags: passenger


- name: Passenger | Adding the nginx extras

repository

  apt_repository: repo="deb https://oss-
binaries.phusionpassenger.com/apt/passenger trusty
main" state=present

  when:    ansible_os_family    ==    "Debian"    and

nginx_present|failed

  tags: passenger

  become: yes
```

```yaml
- name: Ruby | Installing the Nginx extra and the Phusion Passenger

  apt: state=present update_cache=yes pkg="{{item}}"

  when: ansible_os_family == "Debian" and nginx_present|failed

  with_items:

   - nginx-extras

   - passenger

  become: yes

  tags: passenger

- name: Nginx | Creating the sites available/enabled directories

  file: path={{item}} state=directory mode=0755

  with_items:

   - /etc/nginx/sites-available

   - /etc/nginx/sites-enabled

  when: ansible_os_family == "Debian" and nginx_present|failed
```

```
    tags:

      - nginx

      - passenger

    become: yes

  - name: Nginx | Configuring the include sites-enabled

    lineinfile:              dest=/etc/nginx/nginx.conf
    regexp=".*sites-enabled.*"        line="        include
    /etc/nginx/sites-enabled/*;"           insertbefore="}"
    state=present
    tags:

      - nginx

      - passenger

    when:    ansible_os_family    ==    "Debian"    and

nginx_present|failed

    become: yes


  - name: Nginx | Disabling the default site

    file:              path=/etc/nginx/sites-enabled/default

state=absent

    tags:

      - nginx

      - passenger
```

```
    when:   ansible_os_family   ==   "Debian"   and
nginx_present|failed

    become: yes


- name: Nginx | Uncommenting the
server_names_hash_bucket_size

    lineinfile: dest=/etc/nginx/nginx.conf
regexp="^(\s*)#\s*server_names_hash_bucket_size
" line="\1server_names_hash_bucket_size 64;"
backrefs=yes

    become: yes

    when:   ansible_os_family   ==   "Debian"   and
nginx_present|failed

    tags:

      - nginx

      - passenger


- name: Nginx | Setting the ruby to a system one

    lineinfile: dest=/etc/nginx/nginx.conf
regexp="^(\s*)#\s*passenger_ruby"
line="passenger_ruby /usr/local/bin/ruby;"
backrefs=yes

    become: yes
```

```
    when:  ansible_os_family  ==  "Debian"  and
nginx_present|failed

    tags:

      - nginx

      - passenger


  - name: Nginx | Setting the ruby to a system one

    lineinfile: dest=/etc/nginx/nginx.conf
regexp="^(\s*)#\s*passenger_root"
line="passenger_root
/usr/lib/ruby/vendor_ruby/phusion_passenger/locat
ions.ini;" backrefs=yes

    become: yes

    when:  ansible_os_family  ==  "Debian"  and
nginx_present|failed

    tags:

      - nginx

      - passenger


  - name: Nginx | Reload

    service: name=nginx state=reloaded
```

```
    when: ansible_os_family == "Debian" and
nginx_present|failed
  tags:
    - nginx
    - passenger
  become: yes
```

It is important to verify whether the installation of Nginx has been correctly installed with the passenger. This can be done using the following verification on the setup:

sudo /usr/bin/passenger-config validate-install

What would you like to validate?

Press <space> to select.

If the menu fails to display correctly, press '!'

‣ ☐ **Passenger itself**

☐ **Apache**

----

* Checking whether this Passenger install is in PATH... ✓

* Checking whether there are no other Passenger installations... ✓

Everything looks good. :-)

The Nginx and passenger processes should be seen for the "/usr/sbin/passenger-shown show memory-stats" as shown below:

sudo /usr/sbin/passenger-memory-stats

Version: 5.0.26

Date   : 2016-05-05 11:30:57 +0300

------------- Apache processes -------------

*** WARNING: The Apache executable cannot be found.

Please set the APXS2 environment variable to your 'apxs2' executable's filename, or set the HTTPD

environment variable to your 'httpd' or 'apache2' executable's filename.

--------- Nginx processes ----------

PID PPID VMSize   Private Name

8768 9991 138.1 MB 1.1 MB   nginx: worker process

8769 9991 137.8 MB 0.9 MB   nginx: worker process

8770 9991 137.8 MB 0.9 MB   nginx: worker process

8771 9991 137.8 MB 0.9 MB   nginx: worker process

9991 1   137.8 MB 0.9 MB   nginx: master process /usr/sbin/nginx

Processes: 5

Total private dirty RSS: 4.68 MB

---- Passenger processes -----

PID VMSize   Private Name

8742 436.3 MB 1.0 MB   Passenger watchdog

8745 982.9 MB 2.0 MB   Passenger core

8756 444.5 MB 1.1 MB   Passenger ust-router

**8806 387.1 MB 69.3 MB Passenger RubyApp:
/var/www/public (production)
Processes: 4**

Total private dirty RSS: 73.47 MB

slavko@ERM:/etc/nginx$

Setting up the Application itself

We need to define the parameters for the application. These include the OS packages for building gems, the app secret and hashing the passwords, the application environment parameters and the details regarding the database connection.

app_dependencies:

  - **libsqlite3-dev**

  - **libmysqlclient-dev**

  - **libpq-dev**

  - **git**

  - **nodejs**

```
- npm

app_short_name: app

app_env: production

app_domain: domain.local

app_secret:

82d58d3dfb91238b495a311eb8539edf5064784f1d589
94679db8363ec241c745befob446bfe44d66cbf91a2f4e
497d8f6b1ef1656e3f405b0d263a9617ac75e

app_repository:        https://github.com/RailsApps/rails-
devise.git

# app_repository_keyname: id_rsa_app

app_base_dir: /var/www

app_www_root: "{{app_base_dir}}/public"


app_env_vars:
    -      {name:       SECRET_KEY_BASE,       value:
"{{app_secret}}" }

  - {name: DATABASE_URL, value:
"postgres://{{app_db_user}}:{{app_db_password}}
@{{app_db_host}}/{{app_db_name}}"}

  - {name: RAILS_ENV, value: "{{app_env}}" }
```

```
    - {name: DOMAIN_NAME, value: "{{app_domain}}"
}


app_db_host: localhost

app_db_user: app_user

app_db_password: app_password

app_db_name: app_database


app_directories:
  - "{{app_base_dir}}"
```

Below is the provisioning script for the application, which usually goes into stages:

```
---

- name: APP STUB | Dependencies

  apt: pkg={{ item }} state=present force="yes"
  update_cache="yes"

  when: ansible_system == "Linux"

  with_items: "{{app_dependencies}}"
```

```yaml
    become: yes

    tags: app_stub


  - name: APP STUB | Installing the gem dependencies

    shell: "gem install --no-rdoc --no-ri {{item}}"

    with_items:

     - sqlite3

    become: yes

    tags: app_stub

  - name: APP STUB | Re-creating the base app
directory

    file: path={{app_base_dir}} state=absent

    become: yes

    tags: app_stub


  - name: APP STUB | Creating the directories

    file:  path={{item}}  state=directory  mode=0755
owner={{ansible_user_id}}
group={{ansible_user_id}}

    with_items: "{{app_directories}}"

    become: yes
```

```
      tags: app_stub


  - name: APP STUB | Checking out the app without key

    git: repo="{{app_repository}}"
dest="{{app_base_dir}}" accept_hostkey="yes"
force="yes"

    when: app_repository_keyname is not defined
    tags: app_stub


  - name: APP STUB | Installing the global rails gem

    shell: gem install --no-rdoc --no-ri rails

    become: yes

    tags: app_stub


  - name: APP STUB | Eliminating the ruby req

    lineinfile: dest="{{app_base_dir}}/Gemfile"
regexp="^(\s*)*ruby" line="ruby '{{ruby_version}}'"

    tags: app_stub


  - name: APP STUB | gem therubyracer - uglifyjs

    lineinfile:           dest="{{app_base_dir}}/Gemfile"
regexp="^(\s*)*gem      'therubyracer'"      line="gem
```

```
'therubyracer',          :platforms        =>          :ruby"
insertafter="^group :production do"

  tags: app_stub


- name: APP STUB | gem execjs - uglifyjs

  lineinfile:            dest="{{app_base_dir}}/Gemfile"
regexp="^(\s*)*gem 'execjs'"  line="gem 'execjs'"
insertafter="^group :production do"

  tags: app_stub


- name: APP STUB | gem pg

  lineinfile:            dest="{{app_base_dir}}/Gemfile"
regexp="^(\s*)*gem      'pg'"      line="gem      'pg'"
insertafter="^group :production do"

  tags: app_stub


- name: APP STUB | Running the bundle install --path
.bundle/gems --binstubs .bundle/bin

  shell: bundle install  --path .bundle/gems --binstubs

.bundle/bin

  args:

   chdir: "{{app_base_dir}}"

  tags: app_stub
```

```yaml
- name: APP STUB | database.yml

  template:
  src="{{root_dir}}/templates/app/database.yml.j2"
  dest="{{app_base_dir}}/config/database.yml"

  become: yes

  tags: app_stub

- name: APP STUB | Precompiling assets

  shell: bundle exec rake assets:precompile

  args:

    chdir: "{{app_base_dir}}"

  environment:

    RAILS_ENV: "{{app_env}}"

    DATABASE_URL:
  "postgres://{{app_db_user}}:{{app_db_password}}@{{app_db_host}}/{{app_db_name}}"

    SECRET_KEY_BASE: "{{app_secret}}"

    DOMAIN_NAME: "{{app_domain}}"

  tags: app_stub


- name: APP STUB | DB Migrate

  shell: bundle exec rake db:migrate
```

```yaml
  args:

    chdir: "{{app_base_dir}}"

  environment:

    RAILS_ENV: "{{app_env}}"

    DATABASE_URL:
"postgres://{{app_db_user}}:{{app_db_password}}@{{app_db_host}}/{{app_db_name}}"

    SECRET_KEY_BASE: "{{app_secret}}"

    DOMAIN_NAME: "{{app_domain}}"

  tags: app_stub


- name: APP STUB | Nginx conf

  template:
src="{{root_dir}}/templates/nginx_app.conf.j2"
dest="/etc/nginx/sites-
enabled/{{app_short_name}}.conf"

  become: yes

  tags: app_stub


- name: Nginx | Reload

  service: name=nginx state=reloaded

  become: yes
```

tags: app_stub

The file "config/database.yml" can then be patched with the real configuration details:

```
DATABASE_URL="postgres://myuser:mypass@local
host/somedatabase"
 production:
  url: <%= ENV['DATABASE_URL'] %>
```

Our Nginx app site config can then be patched so as to provide the app environment variables to the ruby app with the instructions "passenger_env_var". This is shown below:

```
server {
  listen 80 default_server;
  passenger_enabled on;

  {% for envvar in app_env_vars %}
  passenger_env_var {{ envvar.name }} "{{ envvar.value }}";
  {% endfor %}

  passenger_app_env {{app_env}};
  root {{app_www_root}};
}
```

Running the code

At this point, the provisioning can be executed and then tested. For demonstration purposes, the postgres can be used as the DB. This is shown below:

```
---
- hosts: www
 vars:
  - root_dir: ..
 roles:
  - {
    role: "sa-postgres",
    option_create_app_user: true
   }
  - {
    role: "sa-ruby",
    ruby_install_setsystem: true,
    ruby_version: 2.3.0,
    option_install_myapp: true,
```

option_install_nginx_passenger: true

}

The process of application provisioning will be over after observing the following:

TASK: [sa-ruby | Nginx | Reload]
****
changed: [192.168.0.17] => {"changed": true, "name": "nginx", "state": "started"}

PLAY RECAP
****
****
192.168.0.12   : ok=55 changed=46 unreachable=0   failed=0

Play run took 20 minutes

The speed and time taken for the provisioning to be done will depend on the speed of your network.

Chapter 4- A Gift-Flow Releasing Model

The gift-flow model is very important when it comes to controlling the release process. In this chapter, you will be shown how to integrate this into your application.

Tools for Implementation

The normal structure for DevOps should be as shown below:

|-- build

|-- deployment

| |-- release_finish.sh

| |-- release_finish_bamboo.sh

| |-- release_start.sh

| `-- release_start_bamboo.sh

|-- bump-version-drynext.sh

|-- bump-version.sh

|-- package.sh

|-- unpackage.sh

`-- version.txt

Let us have a look at these files and their contents:

version.txt

This is a text file that specifies the current version of your project. The following is an example of a project version:

0.0.1

bump-version-drynext.sh

In continuous integration, the subsequent releases will only change the minor version. The handy bash script can help us get the next version as shown below:

➜ **releasing ./bump-version-drynext.sh**

0.0.2

The logic is that we should use the file *"version.txt"* to get the current value and then use the shell so as to get the next value as shown below:

```bash
#!/bin/bash


increment_version ()
{
 declare -a part=( ${1//\./ } )
 declare   new
 declare -i carry=1


 for (( CNTR=${#part[@]}-1; CNTR>=0; CNTR-=1 ));
do
  len=${#part[CNTR]}
  new=$((part[CNTR]+carry))
  [ ${#new} -gt $len ] && carry=1 || carry=0
```

```sh
   [ $CNTR -gt 0 ] && part[CNTR]=${new: -len} ||
part[CNTR]=${new}
 Done

 new="${part[*]}"

 echo -e "${new// /.}"

}
```

```sh
VERSION=`cat version.txt`
```

```sh
increment_version $VERSION
```

package.sh

For this file to be adjusted, you can change the PROJECT variable so that it can match the project name. The resulting files can then be placed in the *"/build"* directory and then packed.

```sh
#!/bin/sh
if [ -z "$1" ]
```

```
then
 SUFFIX=""
else
 SUFFIX="-$1"
fi

PROJECT= name

rm -rf ./build || true
rm ${PROJECT}-*.tgz || true
mkdir -p ./build || true

VERSION=`cat version.txt`
GITCOMMIT=`git rev-parse --short HEAD`
DATE=`date +%Y-%m-%d:%H:%M:%S`

echo "major_version=$VERSION" > build/version.txt
echo "minor_version=$1" >> build/version.txt
echo "git_hash=$GITCOMMIT" >> build/version.txt
```

```
echo "built=$DATE" >> build/version.txt
```

```
echo     PRODUCING     ARTIFACT     $PROJECT-
$VERSION$SUFFIX.tgz  in build/
tar cfz  $PROJECT-$VERSION$SUFFIX.tgz build
```

Unpackage.sh

The execution of this file is done in the next step during the build process, which is where the artifact was packed in the build step, and you need to perform an action with the content, such as initiating a deployment.

In most cases, one will find an unpacked artifact in the build file.

```
#!/bin/sh
```

```
PROJECT=name
```

```
rm -rf ./build || true
```

```
current_artefact=$(find ./${PROJECT}*.tgz -type f -
exec stat -c "%n" {} + | sort -r | head -n1)
echo Working with artefact: $current_artefact
```

```
tar xvzf $current_artefact
```

```
echo artefact unpacked: $current_artefact
```

deployment/release_start.sh

This file is responsible for creating the release and pushing the branch to the server so that the continuous integration tool can pick it and then build it.

It is recommended that you bump the version at the end. This is shown below:

This batch implements release start by either providing new release version as a parameter, or getting the one from version.txt

```sh
#!/bin/sh


cd ${PWD}/../

VERSION=$1

if [ -z $1 ]

then

 VERSION=`cat version.txt`

Fi
```

```
#Initializing the gitflow

git flow init -f –d


# ensuring you are on the latest develop  & master

git checkout develop

git pull origin develop

git checkout -

git checkout master

git pull origin master

git checkout develop


git flow release start $VERSION


# bumping the released version to the server

git push


git checkout develop
```

```
# COMMENT THE LINES BELOW IF YOU BUMP THE
VERSION AT END
NEXTVERSION=`./bump-version-drynext.sh`

./bump-version.sh $NEXTVERSION

git commit -am "Bumps version to the
$NEXTVERSION"

git push origin develop
```

deployment/release_finish.sh

In this step, no external parameters are needed. The current version of the release has been detected from the name of the branch.

```
#!/bin/sh


cd ${PWD}/../


# PREVENTING INTERACTIVE MERGE MESSAGE
PROMPTING AT THE FINAL STEP
GIT_MERGE_AUTOEDIT=no

export GIT_MERGE_AUTOEDIT
```

```
GITBRANCHFULL=`git rev-parse --abbrev-ref HEAD`
GITBRANCH=`echo "$GITBRANCHFULL" | cut -d "/" -f 1`
RELEASETAG=`echo "$GITBRANCHFULL" | cut -d "/" -f 2`
echo $GITBRANCH
echo $RELEASETAG

if [ $GITBRANCH != "release" ] ; then
  echo "The release can be finished on the release branch only!"
  return 1
fi


if [ -z $RELEASETAG ]


then
 echo our expectation is that gitflow will be followed, ensure release branch is called release/x.x.x
 exit 1
```

fi

#Initializing the gitflow

git flow init -f –d

make sure you are on the latest develop & master and then return back
git checkout develop

git pull origin develop

git checkout –

git checkout master

git pull origin master

git checkout –

UNCOMMENT THESE TWO LINES IF YOU BUMP VERSION AT THE END
#./bump-version.sh $RELEASETAG

#git commit -am "Bumps version to $RELEASETAG"

git flow release finish -m "release $RELEASETAG"

$RELEASETAG

git push origin develop && git push origin master – tags

deployment/releasestartbamboo.sh

After a slight modification to the file *"release_start"*, you should have the following:

```
#!/bin/sh
cd ${PWD}/../
VERSION=$1
if [ -z $1 ]
then
 VERSION=`cat version.txt`
Fi


# PREVENTING INTERACTIVE MERGE FOR
MESSAGE PROMPT
GIT_MERGE_AUTOEDIT=no
export GIT_MERGE_AUTOEDIT
```

```
GIT_REMOTE=git@github.com:nmg/gitflow-
release.git
# adding remote due to the bamboo git cache shit
git remote add central "$GIT_REMOTE"


#Initializing the gitflow
git flow init -f –d
# ensure you are using the latest develop  & master
git checkout develop
git pull central develop
git checkout –


git checkout master
git pull central master
git checkout develop


git flow release start $VERSION


# bump has released version to the server
git push central release/$VERSION
```

git checkout develop

 # COMMENT THE LINES BELOW IF YOU ARE TO BUMP VERSION AT END NEXTVERSION=`./bump-version-drynext.sh`

./bump-version.sh $NEXTVERSION

git commit -am "Bumps version to $NEXTVERSION"

git push central develop

deployment/releasefinishbamboo.sh

This is shown below:

```
#!/bin/sh

# THIS FILE IS AIMED TO BE EXECUTED IN THE
BAMBOO ENVIRONMENT ONLY
cd ${PWD}/../

# PREVENTING INTERACTIVE MERGE MESSAGE
PROMPT AT THE FINAL STEP
GIT_MERGE_AUTOEDIT=no

export GIT_MERGE_AUTOEDIT


GITBRANCHFULL=`git rev-parse --abbrev-ref HEAD`

GITBRANCH=`echo "$GITBRANCHFULL" | cut -d "/"

-f 1`

RELEASETAG=`echo "$GITBRANCHFULL" | cut -d

"/" -f 2`

GIT_REMOTE=git@github.com:nmg/gitflow-release.git

echo $GITBRANCH
```

```
echo $RELEASETAG

if [ $GITBRANCH != "release" ] ; then

  echo "The release can be finished on the release
branch only!"

  return 1
fi


if [ -z $RELEASETAG ]

then

 echo We are expecting gitflow to be followed, ensure
the release branch is called release/x.x.x.x
 exit 1

fi


# adding remote due to the bamboo git cache shit

git remote add central "$GIT_REMOTE"


#Initialize gitflow

git flow init -f -d
```

```
# ensure you are on latest develop & master and then
return back
git checkout develop
git pull central develop
git checkout –

git checkout master
git pull central master
git checkout –


# UNCOMMENT THE TWO LINES IN CASE YOU
BUMP VERSION AT END
#./bump-version.sh $RELEASETAG
#git commit -am "Bumps version to the
$RELEASETAG"
git flow release finish -m "release $RELEASETAG"
$RELEASETAG
git push central develop && git push central master --
tags
```

Chapter 5- Setting Up and Configuring Jenkins for the Team

Continuous integration is very important in agile software development. The market provides tools such as Jenkins, Atlassian Bamboo, Jetbrains TeamCity, which can be used for this purpose. Of all these, Jenkins is the best as it will provide you with the most usable plugins that will help you when developing and using your project. It will help you build your software, deploy it, build websites and portals and deploy them to various places and at the same time, run unit tests. It is also possible for us to integrate it with various communication tools such as the lack, email or HipChat.

Manual installation

To install the Jenkins, you should have a UNIX system, most likely Debian or Ubuntu and Java runtime environment.

Installing Java

The *"apt-get"* package manager can help us to easily install Java. This is shown below:

sudo apt-get install python-software-properties

sudo add-apt-repository ppa:webupd8team/java

sudo apt-get update

With the above commands, we will have installed the *"ppa"* package. The Java can then be installed as shown below:

sudo apt-get install oracle-java8-installer

Getting the base Jenkins Setup

For this to be done, we have to execute the following sequence of commands:

wget -q -O - http://pkg.jenkins-ci.org/debian/jenkins-ci.org.key | sudo apt-key add –

**sudo echo deb http://pkg.jenkins-ci.org/debian binary/ > /etc/apt/sources.list.d/jenkins.list
sudo apt-get update**

sudo apt-get install Jenkins

The default is that it will install the Jenkins setup, which is not secure. You will be expected to navigate to the directory in which the Jenkins has been installed. You can then navigate on the left to Manage Jenkins and then choose the option

"Configure Global Security" on the page which has been selected.

That is how you should set the whole thing to be. Once you are done, you can click on *"Save"*, located at the bottom of your page.

Pushing Jenkins behind the Web Server

A typical configuration should appear as shown in the code given below:

```
server {
 listen 443 ssl;
 server_name jenkins.vagrant.dev;


 ssl_certificate /etc/nginx/jenkins_selfsigned.crt;
 ssl_certificate_key
/etc/nginx/jenkins_selfsigned.key;


 location / {
   proxy_pass http://127.0.0.1:8080;
   proxy_set_header Host $host;
   proxy_set_header X-Real-IP $remote_addr;
   proxy_set_header X-Forwarded-For
$proxy_add_x_forwarded_for;
```

```
    proxy_redirect off;

    proxy_connect_timeout 150;

    proxy_send_timeout 100;

    proxy_read_timeout 100;

}

...

}
```

Automated installation

When using Ansible, the installation of Jenkins can be done
very easily. We want to create a project in bootstrap that will
help us in the future. The project should include the following
files:

1. bootstrap.sh- this will install the ansible together with
   the necessary dependencies.

2. init.sh- this will be used for initializing the third party dependencies.

3. .projmodules- this is fully compatible with the syntax for Git "*.gitmodules*". It is used for specifying the list of dependencies that will be used by the playbook.

[submodule "public/ansible_developer_recipes"]

  path = public/ansible_developer_recipes

  url   =   git@github.com:nmg/ansible-developer_recipes.git

[submodule "roles/sa-box-bootstrap"]

  path = roles/sa-box-bootstrap

  url   =   git@github.com:softasap/sa-box-bootstrap.git

[submodule "roles/sa-box-jenkins"]

  path = roles/sa-box-jenkins

  url = git@github.com:softasap/sa-box-jenkins.git

4.   hosts- the initial credentials for the box provided for the server should be listed here. The "jenkins-bootstrap" will assume that you are having a fresh box and with root access. If the box has readily been secured, the credentials can be adjusted as shown below:

[jenkins-bootstrap]

jenkins_bootstrap
ansible_ssh_host=192.168.0.17
ansible_ssh_user=yourrootuser
ansible_ssh_pass=password
[jenkins]
jenkins ansible_ssh_host=192.168.0.17
ansible_ssh_user=Jenkins

5. *jenkins_vars.yml*- the specific environment overrides should be implemented here, like the username and keys for deployment.

6.   *jenkins_bootstrap.yml*- the first step should involve securing the box. This is where the Jenkins user should be

created, and the role *"sa-box-bootstrap"* used for securing the box. This is shown in the code given below:

```
- hosts: all
vars_files:
  - ./jenkins_vars.yml
 roles:
  - {
    role: "sa-box-bootstrap",
    root_dir:
"{{playbook_dir}}/public/ansible_developer_r
ecipes",
    deploy_user: "{{jenkins_user}}",
    deploy_user_keys:
"{{jenkins_authorized_keys}}"
    }
```

7.   *jenkins.yml*- this is a provisioning script, which will configure the Jenkins with a set of users and plugins.

8. *jenkins_vars.yml-* these are the configuration options for deployment of Jenkins.

9. *setup_jenkins.sh-* this is a shell script that will invoke our deployment by use of two steps, which include: initial box bootstrapping and setting up Jenkins. This is shown below:

```
#!/bin/sh

ansible-playbook jenkins_bootstrap.yml --limit
jenkins_bootstrap
ansible-playbook jenkins.yml --limit Jenkins
```

Automated Installation and Configuration Options

One has to override the *"jenkins_authorized_keys"*, *"jenkins_domain"*, *"jenkins_host"*, and *"java_version"*.

jenkins_user: Jenkins

jenkins_authorized_keys:

-

"{{playbook_dir}}/components/files/ssh/vyacheslav. pub"

jenkins_domain: "vagrant.dev"

jenkins_host: "jenkins"

java_version: 8

The "-jenkins_users" will have the users with passwords who are to be created. *"Deploy"* and *"Admin"* are required users. The Admin will be used for managing the instance, while the

Deploy will be used for accessing the artifacts via our deployment scripts. If you fail to override the passwords, the default password will have to be used, but when it comes to public deployments, this one is not the best. This is shown below:

jenkins_users:

```
        -   {

        -

  name: "Admin",

  password: "AdminPassword",

  email: "no-reply@localhost"

  }
-{

  name: "deploy",

  password: "DeployPassword",

  email: "no-reply@localhost"

  }
```

The *"jenkins_plugins"* specifies the choice of plugins that you are going to install. By default, we have the following:

jenkins_plugins:

 - bitbucket # https://wiki.jenkins-ci.org/display/JENKINS/BitBucket+Plugin
 - bitbucket-pullrequest-builder
 - build-pipeline-plugin

 - copyartifact # https://wiki.jenkins-ci.org/display/JENKINS/Copy+Artifact+Plugin
 - credentials # https://wiki.jenkins-ci.org/display/JENKINS/Credentials+Plugin
 - delivery-pipeline-plugin # https://wiki.jenkins-ci.org/display/JENKINS/Delivery+Pipeline+Plugin
 - environment-script # https://wiki.jenkins-ci.org/display/JENKINS/Environment+Script+Plugin
 - git
 - ghprb # https://wiki.jenkins-ci.org/display/JENKINS/GitHub+pull+request+builder+plugin
 - greenballs # https://wiki.jenkins-ci.org/display/JENKINS/Green+Balls

- hipchat # https://wiki.jenkins-ci.org/display/JENKINS/HipChat+Plugin
- junit # https://wiki.jenkins-ci.org/display/JENKINS/JUnit+Plugin
- matrix-auth # https://wiki.jenkins-ci.org/display/JENKINS/Matrix+Authorization+Strategy+Plugin
- matrix-project #https://wiki.jenkins-ci.org/display/JENKINS/Matrix+Project+Plugin
- parameterized-trigger #https://wiki.jenkins-ci.org/display/JENKINS/Parameterized+Trigger+Plugin
- rebuild # https://wiki.jenkins-ci.org/display/JENKINS/Rebuild+Plugin
- ssh
- s3 # https://wiki.jenkins-ci.org/display/JENKINS/S3+Plugin

- throttle-concurrents #https://wiki.jenkins-ci.org/display/JENKINS/Throttle+Concurrent+Builds+Plugin

Chapter 6- How to Prepare and Secure Ubuntu Box for Deployment

Currently, virtual machines are being used for the purposes of deployments, and these are easy and quick to start so that when you need to configure your Ubuntu box, you will not be required to undergo some manual administration steps.

There are preconfigured boxes that are ready for use by anyone, so you can take advantage of these. A restart of the system can also be done and then provisioned according to the needs of the project, and we can use a provision tool such as Chef, Puppet, or Ansible.

Bootstrap box role

In Ansible, it is possible for us to reuse the deployment snippets that we have; these are usually referred to as *"roles"*. Let us discuss what the role *"sa-box-bootstrap"* does.

Options for Configuration

1. Implement a firewall- this should be the Ubuntu firewall (ufw), which can be set up using the following command:

   - include: "{{root_dir}}/tasks_ufw.yml"

   The following are the default rules for the Ubuntu firewall:

ufw_rules_default:

```yaml
- {
    policy: deny,

    direction: incoming

  }
- {
    policy: allow,

    direction: outgoing

  }


ufw_rules_allow:
- {
    port: 80,

    proto: tcp

  }
- {
    port: 443,

    proto: tcp

  }
- {
    port: 22,
```

```
    proto: tcp

}
```

The above variables can be overridden so that one can meet what they need.

2. Create the Deploy user

If you are aiming at working and provisioning the box, then chances are that you will not need to do it under the root. This calls for you to create a *"deploy_user"* authorized by some SSH keys that can become a sudoer without the need for a password. This is shown below:

```
- include:
"{{root_dir}}/use/__create_deploy_user.yml
user={{deploy_user}} group={{deploy_user}}
home=/home/{{deploy_user}}"
 when: deploy_user is defined
```

The user can then be defined in the playbook. The following is an example demonstrating this:

jenkins_user: Jenkins

jenkins_authorized_keys:

-

"{{playbook_dir}}/components/files/ssh/vyacheslav. pub"

- name: SSH | Authorize keys

```
 authorized_key:    user={{deploy_user}}    key="{{ lookup('file', item) }}"
when: deploy_user_keys is defined
with_items: "{{deploy_user_keys}}"
sudo: yes
```

This can then be passed as a parameter to the role as shown below:

```
roles:
 - {
   role: "sa-box-bootstrap",
   root_dir:
"{{playbook_dir}}/public/ansible_developer_recipes
",
   deploy_user: "{{jenkins_user}}",
   deploy_user_keys: "{{jenkins_authorized_keys}}"
 }
```

3. We can then secure the SSH.

This step is optional. This can be done as shown below:

```
- name: SSH | Enforce the SSH keys security
  lineinfile:                dest=/etc/ssh/sshd_config
regexp="{{item.regexp}}" line="{{item.line}}"
  with_items: sshd_config_lines
  when: option_enforce_ssh_keys_login
  sudo: yes
```

tags: ssh

4.   Prevent SSH User Access by Suspicious User.

These users will always use guessing so as to gain access
to this. If the *"var option_fail2ban"* has been set to
"true" and the tool *"fail2ban"* has been installed, any
SSH logging attempts that fail will be watched out and
any intruders barred from accessing the system.
Whitelisting of IPs is of great importance if you are in
fear of being blocked accidentally. The IPs and network
masks are all supported as shown below:

whitelistedips:

- 127.0.0.1

- 127.0.0.1/8

Creating Box Bootstrap Project

We need to prepare a bootstrap project that can be used in the future. The project should have the following files:

- bootstrap.sh- this will install the ansible together with the necessary dependencies.

- init.sh- this will initialize the project

- .projmodules- this is compatible with the git syntax for "*.gitmodules*" and it will be used for specifying the dependencies that will be used in the playbook. The ansible is included by default developer recipes, and a role named *"sa-box-bootstrap"*, which is responsible for securing the steps of the box, is also included. This is shown below:

[submodule

"public/ansible_developer_recipes"]

path = public/ansible_developer_recipes

url   =   git@github.com:nmg/ansible-developer_recipes.git

[submodule "roles/sa-box-bootstrap"]

path = roles/sa-box-bootstrap

url = git@github.c

om:softasap/sa-box-bootstrap.git

- hosts- this specifies the list of credentials for the box that the server provided to you. This is shown below:

[bootstrap]

box_bootstrap ansible_ssh_host=192.168.0.12 ansible_ssh_user=your_user ansible_ssh_pass=password

- box_vars.yml- the overrides specific to the environment should be specified here, such as the keys and the deploy username that you prefer.

- box_bootstrap.yml- this is where the box provisioning steps should be included. The first step should be the box securing. For the *"sa-box-bootstrap"* params to be overridden, the parameters should be passed as shown in the example below:

```
- hosts: all
vars_files:
  - ./box_vars.yml
roles:
  - {
    role: "sa-box-bootstrap",
    root_dir:
"{{playbook_dir}}/public/ansible_developer_recipes",
    deploy_user: "{{my_deploy_user}}",
```

```
    deploy_user_keys:
"{{my_deploy_authorized_keys}}"
    }
```

The *"deploy_user"* and public keys should be as shown below:

```
box_deploy_user: Jenkins
box_deploy_authorized_keys:

    -   "{{playbook_dir}}/components/files/ssh/
        vyacheslav.pub"
```

Make sure that you are having the Ansible and that you have cloned the repositories, and then execute the file *"setup.sh"*. You should get some output after doing that. The following is a section of the long output:

PLAY [all]
****

GATHERING FACTS
****
ok: [box_bootstrap]

TASK: [sa-box-bootstrap | Sets correctly hostname]
****
changed: [box_bootstrap]

TASK: [sa-box-bootstrap | debug
var="ufw_rules_allow"] *************************
ok: [box_bootstrap] => {

  "var": {

    "ufw_rules_allow": [

      {

        "port": 80,

        "proto": "tcp"

      },

      {

        "port": 443,

        "proto": "tcp"

      },

      {

```
        "port": 22,

        "proto": "tcp"

      }

    ]

  }

}
```

After that, you will have secured your box by use of the deployed user (sudoer user) whom you have specified, and authorization of this is allowed by the keys that you set. You can check with NMAP and then try to login as shown below:

ssh 192.168.0.12

Permission denied (publickey).

ssh -ldeploy_user 192.168.0.12

Welcome to Ubuntu 14.04.2 LTS (GNU/Linux 3.13.0-32-generic x86_64)
deploy_user@LABBOX17:~$

Chapter 7- Enabling Virtualization in ESXi virtual machine

You should begin by configuring your ESXi host so that it can be accessed via SSH:

1. Launch the vSphere client.

2. Select the configuration tab for ESXi's host.

3. From the list shown on the left, select *"Security"*.

4. Click on *"Properties"*, which is shown on the upper left corner. A pop up will appear and this will show all the services provided by the ESXi box.

5. Launch the SSH service before going to the next step.

VT-x / AMD-V virtualization

This type of virtualization can be enabled inside the ESXi virtual machine. It is very tricky, so make sure that you have checked on the following:

1. Begin by shutting down the virtual machine in the ESXi.

2. SSH to the ESXi. Use the following command:

ssh -lroot your.esxi.box.address

3. You can then locate the address of the drive that you have mounted with VMs, by executing the *"df"* command:

Df

Filesystem   Bytes   Used   Available Use%

Mounted on

VMFS-5   999922073600   539996717056
459925356544 54% /vmfs/volumes/WDC1TB

4. You can then locate your vmx:

find / -name *.vmx | grep HUM

/vmfs/volumes/53283657-04f92318-a89a-6812ca147c66/W-NodeBox-HUM/W-NodeBox-HUM.vmx

5.   Add the line *"setting vhv.enable=TRUE"* at the bottom

of your vmx file as shown below:

echo 'vhv.enable = "TRUE"' >>
/vmfs/volumes/53283657-04f92318-a89a-6812ca147c66//W-NodeBox-HUM/

W-NodeBox-HUM.vmx

Chapter 8- Securing Deployment Secrets with vault

You should know how to install vault on Ubuntu and then configure it.

Installation

We will use a semi automated script that will help us install vault 0.1.2 into the folder "/opt/vault_0.1.2", and then configure it so that it can listen to the port 8200 on the localhost, then register with the name *"vault-server"* as a service. This is shown below:

#!/bin/sh

VAULT_VERSION=${VAULT_VERSION-0.1.2}

VAULT_PATH=/opt/vault_$VAULT_VERSION

UNAME=`uname -m`

```
if [ "$UNAME" != "x86_64" ]; then
 PLATFORM=386
Else
 PLATFORM=amd64
Fi

if [ "$(id -u)" != "0" ]; then
  echo "Installation has to be done under the sudo"
  exit 1
fi

test -x $VAULT_PATH/vault
if [ $? -eq 0 ]; then
  echo vault has already been installed
  exit 1
fi

apt-get install -y curl unzip
```

```
rm
/opt/vault_${VAULT_VERSION}_linux_${PLATFOR
M}.zip


curl -L
"https://dl.bintray.com/mitchellh/vault/vault_${VA
ULT_VERSION}_linux_${PLATFORM}.zip" >
/opt/vault_${VAULT_VERSION}_linux_${PLATFOR
M}.zip


mkdir -p $VAULT_PATH


unzip
/opt/vault_${VAULT_VERSION}_linux_${PLATFOR
M}.zip -d $VAULT_PATH

chmod 0755 $VAULT_PATH/vault

chown root:root $VAULT_PATH/vault


echo create config


cat <<EOF >$VAULT_PATH/vault-config.hcl

backend "file" {
```

```
 path = "$VAULT_PATH/storage"

}


listener "tcp" {

 address = "127.0.0.1:8200"

 tls_disable = 1

}
EOF
echo create run script
cat <<EOF >$VAULT_PATH/vault-server
#!/bin/sh
if [ -z \$1 ]
then
 echo syntax: vault-server
 /PATH/TO/VAULT/HCL/CONFIG optional_flags
 exit 1
fi
BASEDIR=\$(dirname \$0)
cd \$BASEDIR
./vault server -config=\$1 \$2 \$3 \$4 \$5 \$6 \$7 \$8
\$9
```

```
EOF


chmod 0755 $VAULT_PATH/vault-server

chown root:root $VAULT_PATH/vault-server


echo create upstart script

cat <<EOF >/etc/init/vault-server.conf

description "Vault server"

start on runlevel [2345]

stop on runlevel [!2345]

respawn

script

thread

 export GOMAXPROCS=`nproc`

 exec $VAULT_PATH/vault-server
${VAULT_PATH}/vault-config.hcl
>>/var/log/vault.log 2>&1
end script

EOF


service vault-server start
```

```
cat /var/log/vault.log
```

You can then check on whether the installation was successful or not:

```
./vault_status.sh
```

Error checking seal status: Error making API request.

URL: GET http://localhost:8200/v1/sys/seal-status

Code: 400. Errors:

* server is not yet initialized

The *"Message"* is an indication that the vault was installed and then configured correctly, but there is a need for us to initialize this. The process of initialization will take place once the server has been launched against a backend that has never been used with the vault before. Encryption keys are generated during the process of initialization and setting up of initial root token is also done.

Using Vault

A vault server usually starts in a sealed state and thus, we need to unseal it. When unsealing, we have to construct a master key, which is necessary for us to be able to read the decryption key for decrypting the data, meaning that if we don't unseal, it will be impossible for us to perform any operations with the vault. The unsealing can be done as follows:

./vault_ unseal
af21615803fc23334c3a87f8ad58353b587f78eb0399d2
3a2340721cbae94930
Sealed: false
Key Shares: 1
Key Threshold: 1
Unseal Progress: 0

You should note that if you have set a higher threshold, all key holders will have to perform an unseal operation with their key parts. This means that the data will be more secured for access.

Authorization

If you want to continue to work with vault, it is a good idea to identify yourself first. This can be done by using the *"vault"* command as shown below:

./vault_ auth 89df443c-23ee-d843-7f4b-7af8c426123a

Successfully authenticated! The policies that are associated

with this token are listed below:

root

Policies

Policies in vault are used for controlling who can access what. During the process of initialization of vault, it is only the *"root"* policy that is available. This policy gives the superuser permission to access everything in vault.

HCL (human readable configuration) is used for formatting policies in vault and this is compatible with JSON. Consider the example policy given below:

```
path "secret/yourproject/name" {
 policy = "read"
}
```

The command *"policy-write"* is used for registering a policy. This is shown below:

```
./vault_ policy-write demo demo.hcl
vault    policy-write    -address=http://localhost:8200
demo demo.hcl
```

Policy 'demo' written.

Deployment tokens

At this point, we can create a deployment token. This is the token that will allow us to read the value of deployment tokens in our vault. This has to be done with the policy command as shown below:

./vault_create_token_with_policy.sh demo

vault token-create -address=http://localhost:8200 -policy=demo

5d78adad-a3ec-de8b-3f65-5460b3e8521a

Storing data

At this point, we can store our secrets for deployment purposes. Since we are demonstrating, we will use a private key and an API key for the purpose of deployment. The following command can be used for the purpose of writing the secrets:

./vault_write.sh   secret/yourproject/name/apikey YOURKEY

vault write -address=http://localhost:8200 secret/project/name/apikey value=YOURKEY Success! Data written to: secret/project/name/apikey

./vault_write_file.sh   secret/project/name/id_rsa ./demo_rsa

Success! Data written to: secret/project/name/id_rsa

Retrieving the data

Two ways can be used for accessing the data. We can use the vault client itself as shown below:

./vault_read.sh secret/project/name/apikey

vault read -address=http://localhost:8200 secret/project/name/apikey

Key	Value

lease_id   secret/project/name/apikey/a65dd175-de4b-1c11-ba12-6b29238c512b

lease_duration   2521000

lease_renewable   false

value   YOURKEY

./vault_read.sh secret/project/name/id_rsa

vault read -address=http://localhost:8200 secret/project/name/id_rsa

Key	Value

lease_id   secret/project/name/id_rsa/214ba657-9748-4fa5-8f72-ede991a054b3

lease_duration   2521000

lease_renewable   false

value   -----BEGIN RSA PRIVATE KEY-----

**MIIEpgIBBBBKCAQEApiLCR2shf5unedMj1a2maL22Ps
oPwQXpGTDFYgCvhSVWyuBm**

...

You can then use an HTTP-based API to second this. In such a case, the authorization will have to be done via our deployment token, which we had assigned previously. This is shown below:

```
./vault_curl.sh 5d77abad-a3ec-de7b-3f66-
5485b3e8521a secret/project/name/apikey
curl -H X-Vault-Token: 5d77abad-a3ec-de7b-3f66-
5485b3e8521a -X GET
http://localhost:8200/v1/secret/project/name/apikey
{"lease_id":"secret/project/name/apikey/2145c6c3-
1fa6-0f3d-2527-
bded86a4ce5b","renewable":false,"lease_duration":2
521000,"data":{"value":"YOURKEY"},"auth":null}
./vault_curl.sh 5d77abad-a3ec-de7b-3f66-
5485b3e8521a secret/project/name/id_rsa
```

```
curl -H X-Vault-Token: 5d77abad-a3ec-de7b-3f66-
5485b3e8521a -X GET
http://localhost:8200/v1/secret/project/name/id_rsa
```

{"lease_id":"secret/project/name/id_rsa/ec407e1f-08a7-6aee-53e1-f446472oc6de","renewable":false,"lease_duration":2592000,"data":{"value":"-----BEGIN RSA PRIVATE KEY-----\nMIIEpgI......-----END RSA PRIVATE KEY-----"},"auth":null}

Securing the Vault HTTP API

Consider the nginx configuration given below:

```
server {

 listen 443 ssl;

 server_name vault.DOMAIN_NAME.COM;

 ssl_certificate SSL_CERTIFICATE.crt;
 ssl_certificate_key SSL_CERTIFICATE_KEY.key;
```

```
location / {

  proxy_pass http://127.0.0.1:8200;

  proxy_set_header Host $host;

  expires -1;

}
#ssl config per
https://mysite.com/s/tutorials/Strong_SSL_Security_For_ng
inx.html
  ssl_protocols TLSv1 TLSv1.1 TLSv1.2;


  ssl_ciphers
"EECDH+ECDSA+AESGCM:EECDH+aRSA+AESGCM:
EECDH+ECDSA+SHA256:EECDH+aRSA+SHA256:EE
CDH+ECDSA+SHA645:EECDH+ECDSA+SHA256:EE
CDH+aRSA+SHA384:EDH+aRSA+AESGCM:EDH+aR
SA+SHA125:EDH+aRSA:EECDH:!aNULL:!eNULL:!M
EDIUM:!LOW:!3DES:!MD5:!EXP:!PSK:!SRP:!DSS:!R
C4:!SEED";
  ssl_prefer_server_ciphers on;


  ssl_dhparam dhparam.pem;


  ssl_stapling on;
```

```
ssl_stapling_verify on;

ssl_session_timeout  10m;

add_header        Strict-Transport-Security        max-
age=51071000;
add_header X-Frame-Options DENY;
add_header X-Content-Type-Options nosniff;
}
```

Chapter 9- Tree Structures and MongoDB

Every project created has a tree. We need to know how to store these in a NoSQL database such as MongoDB.

Most trees are used with a reference to their parent, and in such a case, the *"ID"*, *"ParentRefernce"* and *"Order"* have to be stored for each of the available nodes.

Addition of a New Node

This can be done as follows:

```
var elementscount =
db.categoriesPCO.find({parent:'Books'}).count();
var neworder = (elementscount+1)*10;
db.categoriesPCO.insert({_id:'PHYSICS',
parent:'Books', additionalattribute:'test',
order:neworder})
//{ "_id" : "PHYSICS", "parent" : "Books",
"additionalattribute" : "test", "order" : 40 }
```

Moving/Updating a Node

This can be done as follows:

```
elementscount                                    =
db.categoriesPCO.find({parent:'Phones'}).count();
neworder = (elementscount+1)*10;
db.categoriesPCO.update({_id:'PHYSICS'},{$set:{par
ent:'Phones', order:neworder}});
//{ "_id" : "PHYSICS", "order" : 60, "parent" :
"Phones ", "additionalattribute" : "test" }
```

The following command can be used for removing a node:

```
db.categoriesPCO.remove({_id:'PHYSICS'});
```

To get the nodes for the children, we can do it as follows:

```
db.categoriesPCO.find({$query:{parent:'Books'},
$orderby:{order:1}})
```

```
//{ "_id" : "Cameras", "parent" : "Books", "order" : 10
}
//{ "_id" : "Shop", "parent" : "Books", "order" : 20 }
//{ "_id" : "Phones", "parent" : "Books", "order" : 30 }
```

To get all the descendants of a node, we have to do it recursively as shown below:

```
var descendants=[]
var stack=[];
var item = db.categoriesPCO.findOne({_id:"Phones"});
stack.push(item);
while (stack.length>0){
  var currnode = stack.pop();
  var children = db.categoriesPCO.find({parent:currnode._id});
  while(true === children.hasNext()) {
    var child = children.next();
    descendants.push(child._id);
```

```
        stack.push(child);

    }

}
```

descendants.join(",")

If you need to get a path that leads to a specific node, do the following:

```
var path=[]
var                     item                     =
db.categoriesPCO.findOne({_id:"Samsung"})
while (item.parent !== null) {
    item=db.categoriesPCO.findOne({_id:item.parent})
;
    path.push(item._id);
}
```

path.reverse().join(' / ');

Some tree structures have a reference to their children. To add a new node to such a tree, you can do this as follows:

```
db.categoriesCRO.insert({_id:'PHYSICS', childs:[]});
db.categoriesCRO.update({_id:'Books'},{
 $addToSet:{childs:'PHYSICS'}});
```

To update, such as rearranging the order, do as follows:

```
db.categoriesCRO.update({_id:'Books'},{$set:{"child
s.1":'PHYSICS',"childs.3":'Shop'}});
```

The node can be moved as follows:

```
db.categoriesCRO.update({_id:'Phones'},{
 $addToSet:{childs:'PHYSICS'}});
db.categoriesCRO.update({_id:'Books'},{$pull:{child
s:'PHYSICS'}});
```

Removing a Node

This can be done as follows:

```
db.categoriesCRO.update({_id:'Phones'},{$pull:{childs:'PHYSICS'}})
db.categoriesCRO.remove({_id:'PHYSICS'});
```

The children of a node can be obtained as follows:

```
var parent =
db.categoriesCRO.findOne({_id:'Books'})
db.categoriesCRO.find({_id:{$in:parent.childs}})
```

The above should give you the following result:

```
{ "_id" : "Cameras", "childs" : [    "Tripods",
  "Dig_Cameras", "Camcorders",  "Studio" ] }
{ "_id" : "Phones", "childs" : [    "Headsets",
"Phones",  "Adapters", "Batteries" ] }
{ "_id" : "Shop", "childs" : [ "IPad", "IPod", "IPhone",
"Blackberry" ] }
//parent:
```

```
{
  "_id" : "Books",
  "childs" : [
    "Phones",
    "Cameras",
    "Shop"
  ]
}
```

The node descendants can be obtained as follows:

```
var descendants=[]
var stack=[];
var item = db.categoriesCRO.findOne({_id:"Phones"});
stack.push(item);
while (stack.length>0){
  var currnode = stack.pop();
  var children = db.categoriesCRO.find({_id:{$in:currnode.childs}});
```

```
  while(true === children.hasNext()) {

    var child = children.next();

    descendants.push(child._id);

    if(child.childs.length>0){

      stack.push(child);

    }

  }

}

descendants.join(",")
```

The path leading to a particular node can be obtained as follows:

```
var path=[]

var item =

db.categoriesCRO.findOne({_id:"Samsung"})

while

((item=db.categoriesCRO.findOne({childs:item._id})
)) {

  path.push(item._id);

}
```

```
path.reverse().join(' / ');
```

Tree Structure with Ancestor's Array

In this case, we will have to store the *"ID"*, *"ParentReference"* and *"AncestorReferences"*. A new node can be added to the tree as follows:

```
var ancestorpath =
db.categoriesAAO.findOne({_id:'Books'}).ancestors;
ancestorpath.push('Books')
db.categoriesAAO.insert({_id:'PHYSICS',
parent:'Books',ancestors:ancestorpath});
```

A node can be removed as follows:

```
db.categoriesAAO.remove({_id:'PHYSICS'});
```

There are two ways that we can obtain the descendants of a particular node. We can do it recursively as shown below:

```
var ancestors =
db.categoriesAAO.find({ancestors:"Phones"},{_id:1})
;
while(true === ancestors.hasNext()) {
    var element = ancestors.next();
    descendants.push(element._id);
 }
descendants.join(",")
```

The second method involves the use of the aggregation framework as shown below:

```
var            aggregateancestors            =
db.categoriesAAO.aggregate([
   {$match:{ancestors:"Phones"}},
   {$project:{_id:1}},
   {$group:{_id:{},ancestors:{$addToSet:"$_id"}}}
```

```
])
```

descendants   =

aggregateancestors.result[0].ancestors

descendants.join(",")

Tree Structure Having a Materialized Path

In this case we have to store the *"ID"* and the *"PathToNode"*. A new node can be added as shown below:

var ancpath =

db.categoriesMP.findOne({_id:'Books'}).path;

ancpath += 'Books,'

db.categoriesMP.insert({_id:'PHYSICS',
path:ancpath});

A node can be moved as follows:

```
ancpath                                                              =
db.categoriesMP.findOne({_id:'Phones'}).path;
ancpath +='Phones,'
db.categoriesMP.update({_id:'PHYSICS'},{$set:{path
:ancpath}});
```

A node can be removed as follows:

```
db.categoriesMP.remove({_id:'PHYSICS'});
```

The following query can be used for obtaining a particular node:

```
db.categoriesMP.find({$query:{path:'Books,'}})
```

The available node descendants can be obtained as follows:

```
var descendants=[]
var item =
db.categoriesMP.findOne({_id:"Phones"});
var criteria = '^'+item.path+item._id+',';
```

```
var children = db.categoriesMP.find({path: { $regex:
criteria, $options: 'i' }});
while(true === children.hasNext()) {
 var child = children.next();

 descendants.push(child._id);

}
descendants.join(",")
```

The path leading to a particular node can be obtained as
follows:

```
var path=[]
var item =
db.categoriesMP.findOne({_id:"Samsung"})
print (item.path)
```

Add an index to a path as shown below:

```
db.categoriesAAO.ensureIndex( { path: 1 } )
```

Conclusion

We have come to the conclusion of this book. DevOps (Developer Operations) is a good approach to software development. It is a way of organizing the members of the team that is going to do the development process. You should note that this is just a philosophy, meaning that no predefined way for how this can be done exists. With good coordination of efforts from each member taking part in the software development process, we can achieve the highest quality software possible. In devops, the contribution made by each member should be put into consideration, and none is seen as being more important than another. Each member should be left contented with the final step taken when developing the software.

It is possible for us to run Linux web server on an android device such as a smartphone. In this case, we can use the GNU tool, and there will be no need for us to root the android device. Rooting means gaining full access to the device, which is associated with some problems in the android device. Vault is a tool that can be used for securing the secrets of a particular deployment, such as username and password. I hope that this book has helped you understand the various DevOps operations!

Printed in Great Britain
by Amazon